Miss Pickerell

Goes to Mars

BY ELLEN MACGREGOR

Cover and illustrations by Paul Galdone

SCHOLASTIC BOOK SERVICES

NEW YORK • TORONTO • LONDON • AUCKLAND • SYDNEY

To Maude I. G. Oliver

for inspiration, encouragement, and fun

Other books by the same author:

Miss Pickerell and the Geiger Counter*
Miss Pickerell Goes Undersea*
Miss Pickerell Goes to the Arctic

Available from Scholastic Book Services

Copyright 1951 by Ellen MacGregor. This edition is published by Scholastic Book Services, a division of Scholastic Magazines, Inc., by arrangement with McGraw-Hill Book Company, Inc.

12th printing .... March 1970

Printed in the U.S.A.

1. MR. HAGGERTY GETS A RIDE

MISS PICKERELL clapped her left hand firmly on top of her hat, to keep it from falling off, and looked up at the huge Ferris wheel turning slowly against the bright blue sky. She watched it rolling back and up and over and down. Back and up and over and down.

The seven children riding in the Ferris wheel screamed delightedly. Miss Pickerell waved up at them, with her free hand.

"Just like a trip to Mars," said the man in a yellow sweater who was running the Ferris wheel. "You're really sure you don't want to try it?"

"My good man!" said Miss Pickerell. "I have told you six times already that I do not want to go up in your Ferris wheel."

At the very thought of such a thing, Miss Pickerell shuddered, and closed her eyes. Miss Pickerell didn't even like to get up on a stepladder. It made her dizzy.

"Quite a family you have there," said the man. "All yours?"

"Certainly not!" said Miss Pickerell. "And thank goodness! They are only my nieces and nephews."

The man in the yellow sweater pulled a lever and stopped the Ferris wheel for a moment. Then he started it once more, and the children screamed again.

"Noisy, aren't they?" said the man.

"Very," said Miss Pickerell. "Sometimes I think I can hardly stand it. Besides that, they *talk* so much."

"They live with you?"

"No, no!" said Miss Pickerell, impatiently. "They live with their father and mother. Their father is my brother."

"Oh," said the man.

"What I mean is," said Miss Pickerell, "I've been visiting them. Their father was too busy to bring them to ride on the Ferris wheel, and—well—I didn't like to see them be disappointed, so I said I would bring them."

"Very kind of you," said the man. "You're really sure you wouldn't like to go up?"

"My good man!" said Miss Pickerell. "You don't seem to be able to understand that I have no intention of getting up above the surface of the earth. All I want is to return my nieces and nephews to their home, so that I can take my cow back to my own farm, and get my rock collection ready for the state fair."

"Your cow?"

"I am very fond of my cow," said Miss Pickerell. "I never go anywhere without her, if I am going to be away from home for long. I wouldn't want her to be lonesome. I was all ready to start home today to get my rock collection ready for the state fair, when this had to happen. I just love rocks."

"What had to happen?" asked the man.

"You," Miss Pickerell said. "You and your Ferris wheel."

The man took his hand from the lever and pointed out across the parking lot beside them.

"It's too bad you don't have a little red trailer for your cow to ride in," he said. "Like that one out there in the parking lot, fastened to the back of that beaten-up old black car."

"For your information," Miss Pickerell said, "that beaten-up old car, as you call it, is in perfect running condition. I have had that car for eighteen years and it has never given me the slightest mechanical difficulty. Furthermore, that *is* my little red trailer. Did you suppose I carried my cow in the back seat?"

The man pulled back on the lever and stopped the Ferris wheel.

"I think the ride's over," he said.

Miss Pickerell bought balloons and pink cotton candy for her nieces and nephews and took them home again as fast as she could. There was just barely room for all seven of them to ride in Miss Pickerell's car, and, as usual, they all talked at once.

When they reached her brother's home, Miss Pickerell loaded her cow into the little red trailer, said good-by all around to her nieces and nephews and her brother and his wife, and then she started out for her own quiet farm on the other side of Square Toe Mountain.

If Miss Pickerell hadn't been so worried about her cow, she would have been quite happy as she jounced sedately along the narrow country road, with her hands held tight on the steering wheel, and her cow swaying gently from side to side in the little red trailer behind the car.

But Miss Pickerell *was* worried about her cow. Her

3

cow seemed unhappy. She seemed sick. Miss Pickerell hoped it was only homesickness.

Once, Miss Pickerell stopped to make sure that her cow was as comfortable as possible. And once, seeing an unusual blue-green rock in the middle of a field, she stopped again and knocked off a small piece with the little hammer she always carried with her.

"It's beautiful," she said to herself, holding the piece of rock in her hand. Miss Pickerell loved rocks.

When she climbed back into her car, she noticed, at some distance ahead of her, a man in a bright blue suit, with an enormous brief case in his hand, standing by the edge of the road.

She had barely started her car again, when a large bus came whizzing past her from behind. The man by the side of the road wildly waved his brief case. But without even slowing down, the bus rushed past, leaving the man standing there.

"I saw what happened," said Miss Pickerell, when she had driven ahead to where the man was. "If you are going in the direction of Square Toe Mountain, I would be glad to allow you to ride with me, on condition—"

"Oh, thank you! Thank you!" said the man. He opened the door of the car and put his large brief case into the front seat. He climbed in beside Miss Pickerell. "You see, it is very important—"

"I was going to say," said Miss Pickerell, making no move to start the car, "that if I take you with me, I must insist that you do not talk. I have had just about as much talking as I can stand for a while. You see, I have been visiting my brother. My brother has seven children."

"I quite understand," said the man. "I merely wanted to remark—"

Miss Pickerell sat perfectly still in the motionless car.

"I'll keep still," said the man.

"That's better," said Miss Pickerell. She stepped on the starter.

"The only thing is—" the man said.

Miss Pickerell turned off the engine.

"I won't say another word," said the man.

Miss Pickerell started the car.

After a few moments, the man took a pair of glasses from the breast pocket of his coat, put them on, and leaned forward to study the speedometer.

"Excuse me," he said, "for speaking. But I have just calculated that, at our present rate of speed—15 miles an hour—it will be thirty-two minutes after five before we reach Square Toe Mountain. Since it is very important for me to be there as soon as possible, I wonder if I might ask you to—"

"I am afraid," said Miss Pickerell, slowing down to 10 miles an hour, "that I shall have to let you out, if you insist on talking. I don't think you quite understand what a strain I have been under this last month. I am not used to having people around. I live all by myself on my little farm. I am not accustomed to the incessant chatter of seven nieces and nephews. Though, of course, I *am* very fond of them."

"I'm sorry I mentioned it," said the man. He sat perfectly rigid, balancing his brief case on his knees, which were jiggling from the vibrations of the floorboards. "I promise I won't speak to you again."

This made Miss Pickerell feel that she was being a little unkind. She had just introduced herself, when an airplane swooshed through the air above them.

Instantly the man leaned over the door of the car and looked up. He seemed very worried.

"It's a jet plane," Miss Pickerell explained. "You can always tell a jet plane by the way it sounds."

"Yes, I know," said the man, pulling his head back in. "And my name is Haggerty. Are you a licensed pilot, Miss Pickerell?"

"Mercy, no!" said Miss Pickerell.

"But you knew that was a jet plane, just by the sound."

"That's on account of my nieces and nephews talking all the time," said Miss Pickerell. "I pick up things like that from their conversation."

"I'm awfully sorry I forgot about talking," said Mr. Haggerty.

"Mr. Haggerty," Miss Pickerell said, "I think I should explain to you why I can't go any faster. It's on account of my cow. She's not feeling well. Besides, my car won't go over 20 miles an hour."

Mr. Haggerty turned around in the seat and looked back to the trailer behind.

"What a beautiful fawn-colored animal!" he said. "A Jersey, I presume?" Then he asked Miss Pickerell how many nieces and nephews she had.

"Didn't I tell you?" Miss Pickerell said. "There are seven. I go every year to visit them for a month, but I'm not sure I shall go again. They talk so much I don't even get a chance to think about getting my collection of rocks ready for the state fair. Last year, they talked about nothing but flying saucers. This year, all they talked about was airplanes. I suppose that's an improvement. At least there *are* such things as airplanes. Airplanes actually exist."

"You do not believe in flying saucers, Miss Pickerell?"

"Why, Mr. Haggerty! No intelligent person believes in flying saucers."

Mr. Haggerty was silent for a moment. "Do you believe in flight through space, Miss Pickerell?"

"Through space?" said Miss Pickerell. "Where to?"

"To places like—the moon, or Mars, maybe."

"Oh, pooh!" said Miss Pickerell. She speeded the car up until the speedometer showed 17 miles an hour.

"Miss Pickerell," said Mr. Haggerty cautiously, "is it all right if I say one thing more?"

"Oh, go ahead!" said Miss Pickerell. "What is it?"

"Would it surprise you to know that I myself, if all goes well, will soon be making a trip to Mars?"

"It would surprise me very much," Miss Pickerell said, "if I believed it. Which of course I don't. No sensible person believes such a thing."

Mr. Haggerty continued. "Perhaps you yourself will some day travel to Mars, Miss Pickerell. It's not at all unlikely."

"Pooh!" said Miss Pickerell.

But Mr. Haggerty had roused her curiosity. She was curious about what kind of man could believe such impossible things.

"Just who are you, Mr. Haggerty?" she asked. "What do you do, anyway?"

"I don't like to brag," said Mr. Haggerty, "but I have a very special kind of brain. That is why I have been sent for to join a scientific expedition which has set up its headquarters near Square Toe Mountain. You see, I am very good at—"

"Excuse me," said Miss Pickerell. She had just heard her cow mooing in the trailer. "I must stop and see if my cow is all right."

But before she could do this, Miss Pickerell's car, for the first time in eighteen years, broke down. Dreadful clunking noises came from its insides.

Miss Pickerell steered to the edge of the road and stopped.

2. A BREAKDOWN

BEFORE Miss Pickerell could even say, "Oh, dear!" Mr. Haggerty had taken off his bright blue coat and folded it across his brief case.

"I know just what's wrong," he said, rolling up his sleeves. "Where do you keep your tools?"

Miss Pickerell told him they were under the back seat, and that she thought he was very kind to do this. Then she got into the trailer with her cow, while Mr. Haggerty was squirming around on his back under the car.

Miss Pickerell could see that the cow was sicker than she had been before. She patted the cow's neck encouragingly.

"We'll be home before long," she said. "You'll feel better after you get back to your own quiet pasture."

"There! It's all fixed," Mr. Haggerty announced, emerging from under the car. He looked into the trailer.

"I love animals," he said. "Especially farm animals."

Miss Pickerell gave a final pat to her cow and climbed out of the trailer.

Mr. Haggerty replaced the tools under the back seat, rolled down his sleeves, and put his coat back on again.

"I had always planned to study veterinary medicine," he said, "but when I got to college, they gave me an aptitude test and discovered about my brain. So I studied higher mathematics instead."

"What about your brain?" Miss Pickerell asked, as she took her place at the steering wheel.

"Well, as I said, I don't like to brag. It's nothing to be especially proud of. I'd much rather be a veterinarian than what I am." He got into the car.

"What *are* you, Mr. Haggerty?"

"Well, you see, I am very quick at scientific calculations. I am in great demand wherever difficult scientific calculations must be made rapidly. That is why I have been sent for to join the scientific expedition near Square Toe Mountain."

Miss Pickerell started the car. "Why, Mr. Haggerty!" she said, when they had driven a little way. "What have you done! We're actually going 25 miles an hour!"

"It was nothing," said Mr. Haggerty modestly.

"You must be a very valuable man to have on an expedition," said Miss Pickerell, "if you can calculate things and fix things too. How soon do you calculate we will reach Square Toe Mountain at this rate, Mr. Haggerty?"

Mr. Haggerty did not hesitate. "At fourteen minutes after four," he said. "And I hope it won't be too late."

"Too late for what?"

"I would like to tell you, Miss Pickerell," said Mr. Haggerty, "but I'm afraid I have already said too much. You see, this expedition I am joining is not my own. The captain who is in charge of the expedition wants to keep it secret. He doesn't want people to know about it."

"Is he ashamed of what he's doing?" Miss Pickerell asked. "Is he doing something wrong?"

"Oh, no, indeed!" said Mr. Haggerty. "But there's always the chance that an expedition such as this might

Miss Pickerell gave a final pat to her cow

fail. It's embarrassing if people know you've started out somewhere, and you never get there. Oh, look! Is that Square Toe Mountain up there ahead of us?"

Miss Pickerell said that it was.

"The captain gave me directions," Mr. Haggerty said, "about how to find the expedition. When I get to a red covered bridge, I'm supposed either to take the left-hand road, or to take the right-hand road, or to go straight ahead. I can't remember which. It's a good thing I wrote it down, isn't it?"

"I'm a little surprised, Mr. Haggerty," said Miss Pickerell, "that you can't remember a simple thing like that —a man with such a good brain as yours."

"That's the way I save wear and tear on my brain," Mr. Haggerty said. "I don't clutter it up with little unimportant things. Anything like that I just write down. And then I forget it. That's why I carry such a large brief case as this—to hold all the things I've written down and forgotten." He unstrapped his brief case and began to go through the mass of notes and papers inside.

"Well, anyway," said Miss Pickerell, "it couldn't be the left-hand road you are supposed to take. That's the road to my farm. Nobody else uses it but me. It's a private road. Nobody else lives anywhere near my farm."

Mr. Haggerty was still fluttering through the contents of his brief case, when they reached the red covered bridge. It was fourteen minutes after four, just as Mr. Haggerty had said it would be.

"This is where I turn off," Miss Pickerell said. "I'll have to let you out here."

Mr. Haggerty picked up his brief case by one strap, and got out of the car.

"You were very kind to give me a ride, Miss Pickerell. Thank you."

"Thank *you* for fixing my car," said Miss Pickerell. "Good-by, Mr. Haggerty. I hope you'll find your directions."

Miss Pickerell was so eager to reach her own quiet farm, and so concerned to know that her cow was not too exhausted from the long trip, that she did not notice the condition of her road.

Otherwise, she might have observed the fresh deep ruts that seemed to indicate that someone had been using her own private road while she was away.

3. MYSTERIOUS VISITORS

M ISS PICKERELL drove through her barnyard and right into the barn, so that her cow could get out of the trailer immediately. She was so concerned about the cow that she didn't even take off her hat before she unloaded her cow, fed her, and milked her.

"Just as soon as I get myself a bite to eat," Miss Pickerell promised her cow, "I'm going to take you down to your pasture for a while. That will make you feel better. I know it will."

She gave the cow an affectionate pat on the neck, and carried the milk pail into the house.

A few moments later, seated in a chair by the window of her quiet, clean kitchen, and drinking a glass of fresh, warm milk, Miss Pickerell thought how good it was to be home. How quiet it was! How restful! How clean!

"That's funny!" Miss Pickerell said to herself. She put her glass of milk down on the kitchen table. "I've been away a whole month, but this kitchen isn't a bit dusty! Well, I'll give the whole house a good cleaning tomorrow, just the same, before I start getting my rock collection ready for the state fair."

She took another drink of milk. Her eyes came to rest on the calendar hanging on the wall beside the telephone. The picture on the calendar showed a girl milking a black-and-white cow.

Suddenly Miss Pickerell jumped so that she almost

spilled her milk. She got up and walked over to the calendar.

"Why, that's the calendar for *this* month!" she said to herself. She remembered distinctly that last month's calendar picture had been of a boy running a green-and-yellow tractor. Miss Pickerell knew perfectly well that she had not changed the calendar before she went away to visit her brother and his family.

"That means," she said slowly, "that somebody has been in my house while I've been gone."

Miss Pickerell went through the whole house, room by room. Every room was as fresh and neat as if it had been cleaned yesterday. Miss Pickerell decided that it *had* been cleaned yesterday.

"Forevermore!" Miss Pickerell said.

It must have been someone who was lost. She was glad whoever it was had found her house.

"I *do* wish they had stayed longer," she thought. "It would be nice to meet such kind, considerate people." She knew instinctively that she would like them.

Miss Pickerell received another shock when she opened her kitchen cupboard to get some cookies to eat with the rest of her milk.

She had expected that her unknown guests would have used some of her food. But her cupboard, which had been almost empty when she left for her visit, was now completely full. The shelves were generously stocked with all kinds of prepared foods in cans and boxes. It was as if someone had bought a great quantity of food all at once, to last a long time. There were even six large purple boxes of pretzels.

Miss Pickerell could make no sense of this. She was vaguely disturbed. Gradually, it began to dawn on her that someone must have been actually living in her house, perhaps for several weeks. This was a very different thing from stopping overnight because of being lost. Miss Pickerell did not like it.

She went out to the barn, and fastening a rope to the cow's halter, led her out into the narrow lane that wound over the top of a small hill and ended at Miss Pickerell's pasture.

As she walked along, Miss Pickerell wished she could get her hands on the people who had been using her house. She'd tell them a thing or two! Why, it was almost like stealing. Even though they had cleaned the house before they left, and even though they had returned all the supplies they had eaten—and more too!

At the top of the hill, Miss Pickerell stopped to catch her breath, and to give her cow a chance to rest. The rope hung slack in her hand.

"You're glad to see your nice quiet pasture again, aren't you?" she said, patting her cow.

The cow mooed plaintively.

When she thought the cow was sufficiently rested, Miss Pickerell pulled gently on the rope, turned around, and started down the hill to the pasture. She stopped with one foot in the air, and her mouth wide open, at the amazing sight spread out before her in the pasture below. "Forevermore!" she said.

4. THE SECRET EXPEDITION

AT THE far end of Miss Pickerell's pasture, a huge, silver-colored structure gleamed in the late-afternoon sun. It was shaped a little like a pencil, but it was much fatter, and had several wide fins at the bottom. Even from here, Miss Pickerell could see that the thing was enormous. It was far bigger than any airplane Miss Pickerell had ever seen or ever heard about. And instead of resting flat on the ground like an airplane, it pointed straight up in the air.

A long thin ladder extended down from the thing to the ground, and even as she looked, Miss Pickerell saw two men walking across the pasture to the ladder. One behind the other, they climbed up and disappeared inside the structure.

For a long moment, Miss Pickerell stood there, shading her eyes with her hand. She was not slow to realize that this must be the secret expedition Mr. Haggerty had been talking about. And or course these must be the people who had been using her house while she was away.

"This is the last straw!" Miss Pickerell said. "Just the last straw!"

She tied the cow to a tree with great angry loopings of the rope, and marched down the lane to the pasture.

A young man dressed in khaki work clothes and a red baseball cap was sitting on the top rail of the fence, beside the pasture gate. He was eating a pretzel.

Miss Pickerell reached out to open the gate.

The young man climbed down from the fence. "I'm sorry," he said, tipping his cap, "but you can't go inside."

"I can too!" Miss Pickerell said. "I am Miss Pickerell. This is my pasture. What is that thing doing in there— that enormous metal contraption?"

"We're going somewhere in it," the young man said. "I'm not supposed to say where."

"That's ridiculous!" said Miss Pickerell. "It's too big to fly. Besides, it's pointing straight up."

"Well, you see, Miss Pickerell, it's not an ordinary airplane."

"That's quite obvious," Miss Pickerell said. "Just what is it, and what's it doing here?"

"It's a space ship."

"Whatever that is!" said Miss Pickerell. "Now I want you to get it out of there immediately. How do you happen to be using this pasture without my permission?"

"Well, you see," the young man said, "we wanted to find some quiet spot where people wouldn't find out what we're doing and bother us. If people knew about it, especially if they knew where we're going, they would ask all sorts of questions. We would have to spend so much time answering questions that we wouldn't have any time to make preparations for our trip. You know how people are!"

Miss Pickerell looked across to the space ship.

"How did you get it in here?"

"We built it. When we found that no one was using this pasture, and that house up there that seemed to be abandoned—"

"That house was *not* abandoned," Miss Pickerell said. "It's *my* house. I was merely away on a visit. You have been trespassing."

"Would you care for a pretzel?" the young man asked. He took a waxed paper package from his pocket and began to unwrap it.

"No, I wouldn't," Miss Pickerell said. "And don't try to change the subject. You will have to leave my pasture immediately. Who's in charge here, anyway?"

"That would be Captain Crandall," said the young man.

Miss Pickerell reached for the gate again, but the young man stepped in front of her and barred the way.

"Captain Crandall is very busy inside the space ship, Miss Pickerell, and he doesn't want to be disturbed."

"It's too bad about Captain Crandall being so busy!" Miss Pickerell said. "Kindly stand aside."

The young man still stood with his back against the gate.

"Under any other circumstances, Miss Pickerell," he said, "I know the captain would be delighted to meet you. However, since we will be taking off any minute now—we are just waiting for another member of our crew to join us—it will be impossible for him to see you. That's why I have been stationed out here. Just to keep people from bothering us at the last minute—in case someone has found out where we're going."

Miss Pickerell turned and pointed up the lane.

"Do you see that cow tied to a tree? That's my cow. She belongs in this pasture. And I'm going to put her there. Before I do, I want all that—all that *stuff* in there

19

"Don't you dare return to this pasture!"

taken away. All those sheds and things, and especially that enormous contraption."

"The captain will be very sorry to miss seeing you, Miss Pickerell. Perhaps later, when we have returned—"

"Don't you *dare* return to this pasture!" Miss Pickerell said. "Now, are you going to tell your captain I want to see him, or aren't you?"

"I tell you what I could do," the young man said. "I might be able to get a message to him."

"Now you're talking sense," Miss Pickerell said.

"As long as I have to report you to the executive officer."

"As long as you have to do what!" Miss Pickerell shrieked.

"Report you. On my walkie-talkie. You see, my orders are to report any suspicious characters. Not that you look like a suspicious character, Miss Pickerell. I didn't mean that at all."

The young man was embarrassed, but Miss Pickerell was far too angry to notice. She was so angry that she choked when she tried to speak, and no words came.

The young man leaned down and took the handset from a walkie-talkie strapped around his chest. He held the handset to his ear.

"You see, Miss Pickerell," he said, "we use this walkie-talkie to talk back and forth to the space ship when we're outside."

"You don't have to explain walkie-talkies to me," Miss Pickerell said. "I've heard all about walkie-talkies from my nieces and nephews. Just turn that thing on and tell your captain I want to see him immediately."

The young man reached down and flipped a switch. "That's funny!" he said. "It doesn't seem to work. Here, hold this phone a minute, will you, so I can use both hands?"

Miss Pickerell held the phone to her ear. She heard a faint click.

"There!" said the young man. "It's fixed. I'll take it now."

But Miss Pickerell saw her opportunity. She inhaled a deep breath and was about to ask to speak to the captain when a sharp crisp voice spoke in the receiver at her ear. "Wilbur. Come here immediately."

Miss Pickerell was so startled that she handed the phone back to the young man, who held it to his ear.

"Yes, Captain," he said. "Coming, Captain. Right away, Captain."

"That was Captain Crandall," he said to Miss Pickerell. "I guess we must be almost ready to start." He replaced the handset on the walkie-talkie and opened the gate.

"When you get inside that thing, Wilbur," Miss Pickerell said, "just tell your captain that I want to see him right away."

Wilbur went through the gate.

Miss Pickerell continued. "Tell him I want to see him up at my farmhouse. I don't know why I should stand around out here waiting for him."

"I'll tell him," Wilbur said, starting for the space ship. "If I get a chance. If he's not too busy."

"Tell him I'll give him half an hour," Miss Pickerell said. "Just half an hour. If he isn't there by then, I'll—

I'll report *him*. That's what I'll do. I'll report him to—
I'll report him to the governor. Maybe you think I don't
know the governor, but every year for fifteen years my
rock collection has won first prize at the state fair, and
one year the governor himself gave out the blue ribbons.
'That's a very fine collection of rocks you have, Miss
Pickerell,' the governor said to me."

"Good-by, Miss Pickerell!" Wilbur called. He was
halfway across the pasture.

"Remember now!" Miss Pickerell shouted. "Just half
an hour!" She turned around and marched up the lane.

"I'll get them out," she said, as she passed her cow.
"I'll get them out of your nice quiet pasture, don't you
worry!"

Miss Pickerell hoped the men would believe her
threat about reporting them to the governor. She hoped
that would make them go away. Actually, Miss Pickerell
was far too much in awe of the governor to do such a
thing. Miss Pickerell would never dream of bothering
the governor with her own private troubles.

5. MISS PICKERELL IS SUSPICIOUS

THE MINUTE Miss Pickerell entered the kitchen, she looked up at the clock on the shelf over the telephone. It was five minutes after five. She was far too angry and upset to want to eat anything. All she could think about was the men in her pasture.

She brought her rock collection out to the kitchen table and began to get it ready to enter in the state fair. But Miss Pickerell couldn't keep her mind on this, either. She kept looking up at the clock, and watching for the captain through the kitchen window. But the captain did not come. Nor did anyone else. Apparently the men were going to defy her. Obviously they were going to stay right there until they got ready to leave, while Miss Pickerell's poor sick cow had to remain outside in the lane, tied to a tree.

Miss Pickerell boiled with the injustice of it.

It was now twenty-five minutes to six. Half an hour had gone by.

Miss Pickerell got some large pieces of white cardboard and a small paintbrush. Then, using the India ink with which she made labels for her rock collection, she lettered several large NO TRESPASSING signs. At least she could put these up and keep anyone else from coming to her pasture!

Miss Pickerell looked again at the clock. "I'll give them five minutes more," she said.

She got some nails for the signs, and took out her favorite hammer—the one that was so easy to use because its head was a magnet and held each nail until the first blow was struck.

If only there were someone she could report the men to!

If she lived in a city, she could simply telephone a policeman and tell him that someone had been living in her house without permission. The policeman would make them go away.

But Miss Pickerell didn't live in the city, and there weren't any policemen to make the men go away. She thought again about the governor, but she knew the governor had much more important things to worry about. The governor wouldn't be interested unless the men were criminals or spies.

Miss Pickerell caught her breath and put her hand to her lips. Perhaps they were criminals or spies! How did she know? Perhaps they were doing something very wrong. They had certainly been most anxious to keep people from knowing what it was. Perhaps she *should* report them to the governor.

Miss Pickerell slipped the magnetic hammer into the commodious pocket of her big apron and crossed the kitchen to the telephone on the wall. She put in a long-distance call for the governor's mansion.

It took quite a while for the call to go through, and as she waited, Miss Pickerell hoped she was doing the right thing. She hoped the governor wouldn't be angry.

It was the governor's wife who finally answered. She

said the governor was busy with a special meeting of his cabinet.

Miss Pickerell tried to explain. She told how she had been away from her home for a month; how she had returned to find someone had been using her house and pasture without permission; how she had discovered the enormous metal structure; how secret the men had been about whatever it was they were doing; and how they refused to leave.

"I was afraid they might be some kind of spies," Miss Pickerell concluded.

"Oh, dear!" said the governor's wife. "That sounds serious. I think I'd better have the governor call you back. He'll be through in an hour or so."

When she had hung up, Miss Pickerell was surprised to find that she was shaking. Now that she had done this thing, she felt a little silly. There wasn't anything more she could tell the governor when he called. Probably the men had a perfectly good reason for whatever they were doing.

On the other hand, they *might* be spies or criminals. It would be an hour before the governor called back. Miss Pickerell decided to see what else she could find out in the meantime.

She put a pink sweater on over her apron and went back to her pasture.

6. AN UNEXPECTED TRIP

T HE PASTURE looked just as it had before, except that Wilbur was not in sight. Miss Pickerell went straight to the gate and opened it. She walked directly to the space ship, her feet scuffing through the grass, and stepped up on the hideous metal and concrete platform that had been built for the space ship to rest on.

Miss Pickerell looked around. No one was in sight. The interlopers must be above in that contraption. She looked up. Only then did she begin to grasp the size of the space ship. It towered above her, and the thin metal ladder leading up to it seemed miles long.

"Yoo hoo!" Miss Pickerell called.

No answer.

"You men!"

There was no response.

Miss Pickerell opened her mouth to call again, and then she closed it, because she had just had a very daring idea.

Suppose one of the men did come down to talk to her. Even if he told her the truth about what they were doing in that thing up there, Miss Pickerell would have no way of knowing whether to believe him.

No, there was only one way to find out what was going on up there, so that she could give the governor an accurate report!

Miss Pickerell closed her eyes and leaned against the ladder. "No, I can't," she whispered to herself. "I just can't. It would make me so dizzy." Again she started to call, and once again she closed her mouth before she had done so.

She grasped one of the rungs of the ladder with her hands. She put one foot on the lowest rung. She stood there a moment with her eyes closed, and then she forced herself to climb to the next rung. She dared not look down. Already she was so dizzy that she thought she would fall. Besides that, the hammer in her apron pocket banged against her leg each time she moved. But she made herself reach up to the next rung. She made herself go on.

Once, when it seemed she was already miles above the earth, she opened her eyes for just an instant and looked up. The space ship still loomed far above her.

"I can't go on," she whispered. Her hands were damp with perspiration, and her head reeled with dizziness. "I'll have to go down again."

At that moment, she heard, coming to her faintly through the air, the sound of her cow mooing. It was almost as if the cow were encouraging her, as if the cow were saying, "You can do it, Miss Pickerell. I know you can."

Miss Pickerell let out her breath and continued to climb.

Just as she thought she could go no farther, her fingers grasped a sort of sill. Miss Pickerell realized that she had reached the space ship.

She dragged herself up to the opening and lay there

Miss Pickerell dragged herself up to the opening

a moment, half in and half out, with her stomach pressed against the sill. She took one look backward at her cow, and as she did so, she saw something else, but she was too agitated from her climb to pay it much attention. What she saw was the blue-suited figure of Mr. Haggerty hurrying down the lane to the pasture gate, his large brief case swinging in his hand.

Miss Pickerell pulled herself through the opening, and through a second doorway just behind it, and then, too weak to stand, she rested for a moment on her hands and knees.

She opened her eyes and looked up. She found herself inside a large, partly circular room. At the far side of this room stood two men, looking up at a large panel with a mass of complicated-looking instrument dials. Nearby, at one side of her, Miss Pickerell saw several curved couches or bunks, with deep springs and cushions.

One of the men at the other side of the room turned his head partly around, as if he might have heard Miss Pickerell come in. She got to her feet, and as she did so, her dizziness overcame her and she collapsed into one of the bunks.

She heard someone say, "Well, there he is at last!"

Someone else called out, "Haggerty! Where in the world have you *been* all this time?"

Miss Pickerell opened her mouth to say that she wasn't Mr. Haggerty, but before she could speak, someone shouted, "Let 'er go!"

There was a heavy clanking sound as the two doors behind her closed. Then there came an ear-splitting hissing and a thunderous rumbling. The bunk beneath Miss Pickerell rose like an explosion. A tremendous force pushed her deep into the springs and cushions of the bunk. She felt as though she would be pushed right through. The force tore away her strength, her breath, everything.

She lost consciousness.

7. MISS PICKERELL IN SPACE

WHEN Miss Pickerell came again to her senses, the pressure was gone, but in place of it was a strange, giddy, light sensation, as if she had no weight at all. Miss Pickerell had never been *this* dizzy in her life. She was frightened. She wondered if she dared to move. She was almost afraid to open her eyes, but she did—just a little.

Across from Miss Pickerell was another curved bunk, similar to the one in which she was lying. A man was sitting in the middle of this bunk. He was shaking his head slowly and going "Tch, tch, tch."

"Lady," he said, "you have absolutely no business being here."

"You had absolutely no business being in my pasture," said Miss Pickerell. "What happened? Was there an explosion?"

"Nothing like the explosion there's going to be when the captain finds out about this!"

"That reminds me," Miss Pickerell said. "I want to see this captain of yours." She moved her arm and started to sit up.

The most amazing thing then happened. The bare movement of her arm lifted her quite out of the bunk where she was lying. The man across from her reached out and pushed her gently back.

"Better fasten that strap across your lap, lady," he said, "if you don't want to float away."

"Stop calling me 'lady,'" Miss Pickerell said. "My name is Miss Pickerell."

"I'm Killian," said the man. "Executive officer of this ship. Hate to think what the captain is going to say when I have to tell him about you."

Miss Pickerell fastened the strap Mr. Killian had indicated. "Thank you, Executive Officer Killian," she said. "This strap does make me feel more secure."

"Just call me Mr. Killian."

Miss Pickerell sat up, and this time she did not float out of her bunk. She saw that Mr. Killian was a middle-aged man with an impassive face and leathery-looking skin. Even in this artificial light, Miss Pickerell could see that his brown hair had faded streaks. Mr. Killian gave her the impression of being a man who had spent most of his life out-of-doors, buffeted by the wind and burned by the sun. But she was concerned at the moment with her own sensations.

"I don't understand what has happened," she said. "Why do I feel so light?"

"Because we're traveling through space."

"But we can't be!" Miss Pickerell said. "We aren't even moving. I can tell by the feeling that we're standing perfectly still."

"Just seems that way," Mr. Killian said. "We're moving, all right. Straight up."

"Forevermore!" Miss Pickerell exclaimed. "You mean we're in the stratosphere?" She had heard from her nieces and nephews about airplanes that fly very rapidly through the stratosphere, high above the earth. "I never imagined the stratosphere was like this! And I never would have thought this—this thing could really take off. It was so big."

"Probably used to airplanes," said Mr. Killian.

"Why, of course I am!" said Miss Pickerell. "I ought to be! I've had to hear so much about them from my nieces and nephews. They'll be *so* interested when I tell them about this big airplane and how it took off pointing straight up into the stratosphere."

"Passed the stratosphere," Mr. Killian said, "long ago."

Miss Pickerell said, "I believe I'll send my nieces and nephews a telegram when we land. How soon will that be, Mr. Killian? And just where are we going, anyway?"

"Be a long, long time before we land," Mr. Killian said darkly, "*if* we ever do; and where we're going you won't be able to send any telegrams."

Miss Pickerell saw something moving out of the corner of her eye. She turned her head and gasped at what she saw. What she saw was the young man Wilbur. But Wilbur was not walking. Wilbur was swimming—yes, actually swimming—right across the room, without even touching the floor. He had emerged from one of two openings in a partition beside the panel of instruments.

"Why, hello there, Miss Pickerell!" Wilbur said. He tipped his cap, and then, instead of putting it back on, he released it from his fingers. The cap remained suspended in the air. "Forevermore!" Miss Pickerell said.

Wilbur turned to Mr. Killian. "Did you tell the captain Miss Pickerell came with us? Was he mad?"

"Haven't told him yet," Mr. Killian said. "Not supposed to interrupt him. Still busy over there in his own compartment. What's he doing in there, anyway?"

"Writing a speech," Wilbur said. "To give when we get back to earth."

"Back to earth!" Miss Pickerell exclaimed. "Why, what are you talking—"

"Might as well save himself the trouble," said Mr. Killian. "Probably never get there now. Not without Haggerty."

Wilbur's face went quite white. He reached up to a ring in the ceiling above him and steadied himself in the air. He spoke in a hoarse, frightened voice. "You mean we left Haggerty behind? Why, Mr. Killian! Who's going to do the calculations for our flight?"

"I'm not," Mr. Killian said flatly. "I don't know how. All I know how to do is tell if we're on our course, or off it. Guess I'd better check the instruments."

He unfastened the strap which had been holding him down, and floated across to the instrument panel. Wilbur, nervous and frightened, swam along close beside him. Neither man paid any further attention to Miss Pickerell.

She thought this extremely rude. They hadn't even given her a chance to tell them that Mr. Haggerty was right down there on the ground, and all they had to do was to go back and get him—if it was so important.

8. THE CAPTAIN GETS A SHOCK

FROM across the room came a low buzz of conversation, where Mr. Killian and Wilbur were floating in front of the instrument panel and earnestly studying various dials and gauges. Miss Pickerell decided this would be a good time to have a talk with the captain. The men might be afraid to interrupt him, but she certainly wasn't.

It seemed quite warm in the space ship, and Miss Pickerell took off her pink sweater and pressed it down against the surface of her bunk. She unclamped the belt across her lap.

At first, Miss Pickerell wasn't quite sure how she should leave her bunk: whether she ought to put her feet out first, or whether she should go head first. And for one awful moment, she thought, "What if the air doesn't hold me up?" But she knew that was silly. If Wilbur and Mr. Killian could swim through the air, she certainly could too.

Miss Pickerell put her hands beneath her and pushed herself up. But this was unnecessary. Now that the belt was unfastened, she simply floated right out into the room. She held her breath.

"Why, it's magic!" she said to herself. "I've never felt anything like this. And I'm not a bit dizzy." She bounced delicately against the ceiling, feeling exactly as if she were a balloon.

In a few moments, Miss Pickerell learned how to guide her movements. The rings she found set at intervals across the ceiling were a help. She noticed, too, that there were handholds all around the circular wall of the room.

The men were conferring at the instrument panel. They seemed so absorbed in their problem as to have forgotten all about Miss Pickerell.

She was about to ask where she would find the captain, when a crisp sharp voice called out, "Mr. Haggerty! Come here immediately."

The voice seemed to come from one of the openings in the partition. Miss Pickerell swam toward it.

"You tell him, Wilbur," she heard Mr. Killian say.

"No, you," said Wilbur. "You're the executive officer."

"Don't bother," Miss Pickerell called out. "I'll explain." She swam through the opening just as the voice was calling again.

"Mr. Haggerty. Come *here!*"

This enclosure was much smaller than the large room. Around its edges were a number of very complicated-looking pieces of equipment, none of which made much sense to Miss Pickerell.

In the middle of this small compartment was an adjustable cushioned chair. The chair was turned with its back to the opening so that all Miss Pickerell could see of the man sitting in it was that he had short iron-gray hair and a fat red neck.

The man called again. "Mr. Haggerty!"

Miss Pickerell, looking down from over the top of his head, saw him angrily unsnap a belt which had been

She had never seen such a startled man

holding him in the chair. He pushed himself up with his hands.

"Careful!" Miss Pickerell said. "Don't bump your head on the ceiling."

The man turned around in the air and stared at her. Miss Pickerell thought she had never seen such a startled man. Beneath the short crew cut of his iron-gray hair, his bright blue eyes bulged wide in his plump red face.

"Good gracious!" he said, almost in a whisper. "Who in the world are you?" And then, even before Miss Pickerell could answer, he shouted, so loud that it hurt her ears, "MR. HAGGERTY!"

"It won't do you any good to shout like that," Miss Pickerell said. "Mr. Haggerty can't possibly hear you from down there on the ground." She steadied herself by holding a ring in the ceiling.

The captain reached out one hand to the chair below him, and with the other, he held his forehead. "This can't be happening!" he said. "It can't really be!" Then he called in a lower tone of voice, "Mr. Killian! Wilbur! Come here."

Mr. Killian and Wilbur floated in immediately.

"Has anybody made the introductions?" Wilbur asked. "Miss Pickerell, this is Captain Crandall."

"How do you do, Captain Crandall," Miss Pickerell said. "I really just came in here to ask you about how soon it will be before I can get home again, and to tell you—"

"Who let this happen?" asked the captain in a stern voice.

"Nobody," Mr. Killian said. "She just got on all by herself."

"That's not what I'm talking about," said the captain. "We'll go into that matter later. What I want to know now is how we happen to have left without Mr. Haggerty."

"It's very easy to understand, Captain Crandall," Miss Pickerell said. "These men just made a very natural mistake. When they heard me get on they thought I was Mr. Haggerty, and started the ship. I don't imagine any real harm's been done, because I saw Mr. Haggerty coming into the pasture just as I got to the top of the ladder. I'm sure he'll wait until you go back for him."

Captain Crandall looked at Mr. Killian. "Are we on our course?"

Mr. Killian nodded. "Guess so. Near as I can tell. But say—"

"Do not address me as 'Say,'" said Captain Crandall.

"Let us try to maintain a little dignity on this voyage—even if we have left our navigator behind, and even if we do have a stowaway."

"Yes, sir," Mr. Killian said. "I only wanted to call your attention, sir, to the instruments."

"What about them?"

"Some of them don't seem to be giving the right readings. If anything happens to the instruments, sir, we're sunk, sir."

"I don't think you need to worry about that," Miss Pickerell said. "I'm sure Mr. Haggerty can fix any instruments that might go wrong. He seems to be very good at that sort of thing. At least he fixed my car very easily. So, as soon as you take me back—"

The captain looked at her icily. "Would you mind keeping still for just a minute, Miss. . . ."

"Pickerell," said Wilbur.

"Miss Pickerell?"

"I'm only trying to help," Miss Pickerell said. "Naturally, I'm sorry if you have been inconvenienced, but it just happens that it wasn't very convenient for me, either. I have a sick cow down there on the ground. Besides that, I want to get my rock collection ready for the state fair. That's one of the reasons I came in here. I wanted to ask you how soon—"

"She talks about inconvenience!" the captain said through clenched teeth. "Miss Pickerell! Do you have any idea at all of the seriousness of what's happened?"

"Only that I think you're making too much of this thing, Captain Crandall. Everybody makes mistakes. It surely can't matter a great deal if you have to go back and make a second start. You'll only be a few hours later getting to wherever you're going."

"A second start, she says!" Captain Crandall held his head with both hands as if he were afraid it might split.

"I don't want to be unreasonable," Miss Pickerell said. "If it's really so important for you to keep right on going, I won't insist that you take me back. But I should think you'd want to go back, on account of Mr. Haggerty."

"Miss Pickerell," Captain Crandall said, "nothing would give me greater pleasure than immediately returning you to wherever it is you came from. Even disregarding the matter of Mr. Haggerty. But the inescapable fact is that we can't go back."

"That's right," Mr. Killian said. "Course was pre-set before we started."

"How ridiculous!" Miss Pickerell said. "If you're using some kind of an automatic pilot, you can certainly turn it off, and pilot the ship yourselves!"

"It's scarcely a question of piloting," Captain Crandall said. "When you start out on such an expedition as ours—when you set out in a space ship to go to another planet—then everything must be very carefully worked out in advance. Even then, something could go wrong with the calculations. That is why we would never have dreamed of starting without Mr. Haggerty."

"What was that you said about a planet, Captain Crandall?"

"Mars is a planet, Miss Pickerell."

"Mars!" Miss Pickerell exclaimed. "Why, Captain

Crandall! I never heard of anything so ridiculous as expecting to get to Mars. Have you ever looked at Mars up in the sky?"

"It happens, Miss Pickerell, that I have made a rather exhaustive study of Mars."

"Then I don't see how you could ever have such a silly idea as trying to go to that tiny little bit of a red star. I know it's called a planet, but it looks just like all the other stars, except that it's redder than most of them. Even the time I saw it through a ten-cent telescope at the state fair, it didn't look any different. Why, Mars must be millions of miles away!"

Mr. Killian said, "I'm going out to look at the instruments."

"Miss Pickerell," Captain Crandall said, "if you come to a good stopping place, I'd like to say a word. Is it your habit to talk constantly?"

"Why, I hardly talk at all," Miss Pickerell said. "I don't usually have anyone to talk *to,* living all alone the way I do. And that reminds me, Captain Crandall, I have a bone to pick with you for trespassing on my farm. Now, as soon as we get back, I want you to——"

A frightened shout from Mr. Killian at the panel of instruments in the larger room interrupted them. Without even excusing themselves, the captain and Wilbur swam rapidly away.

Miss Pickerell sighed. Captain Crandall was certainly a very difficult man. She hadn't settled a thing with him about getting back to her cow and her rock collection.

9. SOMETHING GOES WRONG

MISS PICKERELL waited a few minutes to see if the captain would return.

    At one side of the room, she noticed something that had escaped her attention before. It was a compact metal box with a long thin slit on one side. Every few minutes, a large colored square of paper would emerge from this slit and float out into a mesh container. Miss Pickerell was intelligent enough to realize that this must be some sort of automatic camera which was constantly taking pictures of the ground as they flew. It made her think of the time she had had her picture taken at the state fair, just by putting ten cents in a slot and sitting perfectly still while a light flashed on and then off again.

Miss Pickerell had always wondered what her farm would look like from up in the air. She was about to float over to the pictures and examine them, when she heard Wilbur's voice at the opening behind her.

"Are you all right, Miss Pickerell? I'm just going to get a drink."

This made Miss Pickerell realize that she was thirsty. "I'll come with you," she said, floating around. "Where's the drinking fountain?"

"There isn't any," Wilbur said. "You stay right there. I'll bring your drink."

"What a nice young man!" Miss Pickerell said to herself. She lowered herself into the captain's adjustable chair and snapped the belt to hold herself in, just as Wilbur returned, bringing a strange sort of can with a tube sticking out of it. Miss Pickerell, supposing this to be the handle, reached out to take hold of it.

"Not that way, Miss Pickerell. Put the tube in your mouth."

"How odd!" Miss Pickerell said, as she placed the tube between her lips.

Wilbur said, "Now I'll pump the water into your mouth."

Miss Pickerell said, "Mmm mmm mmm mmm MMM mmm?" She was trying to say, "Why don't I just drink it?" but the tube was in the way.

Wilbur seemed to understand what she meant. "We have to keep our beverages in tight cans like this," he said. "If your drink were in a cup, it wouldn't stay there. It would just float right out of the cup, the way you would float out of your chair, if you weren't belted in."

He began to work a little pump on the bottom of the can, and the cool fresh water spurted into Miss Pickerell's mouth. It tasted delicious.

"Thank you, Wilbur," she said. "But I wish I could understand better. How am I going to explain to my nieces and nephews about this flight if I don't understand it myself? I wish I could understand why I feel so light. I wish I knew why it is possible for us to swim through the air the way we do."

Wilbur swam to the opening and looked out nervously. "I'll try to explain, Miss Pickerell," he said. "But if the captain calls, I'll have to go right away." He came back and balanced himself in the air near Miss Pickerell's

"Why don't I just drink it?"

chair by slipping one finger lightly through a ring in the ceiling.

"We'll start with gravity," he said. "Now, Miss Pickerell, the way gravity works is—"

"I know all about gravity," Miss Pickerell interrupted. "When I hold something in my hand and then let go, it falls. That's gravity."

"Sure," Wilbur said. "But do you know what causes it?"

Miss Pickerell tried to think. "Not exactly," she admitted. "I've never really thought about it. I guess gravity is just one of those things you take for granted."

"It's just the earth pulling against things," Wilbur said. "That's all gravity is."

"You mean like a magnet?" said Miss Pickerell, remembering her magnetic hammer. She slipped her hand into the pocket of her apron to make sure that it was still there, for the hammer was now as weightless as Miss Pickerell's own body.

"That's right," Wilbur said. "Just like a magnet pulling a piece of metal."

"Except," Miss Pickerell said, "that the magnet doesn't work if the piece of metal is too far away from it."

"It's exactly the same with gravity," Wilbur said. "The earth's gravity doesn't work on anything that's too far away from it."

"I never thought about that before," said Miss Pickerell slowly. "But it does make sense. I suppose that's why the stars don't fall down on the earth."

"Yes," said Wilbur, "but what I was really thinking

49

about was this space ship. We're floating through space, with no gravity to hold us back and no air friction to slow us down. That's why you feel so light. That's why we can float in the air. Do you understand now, Miss Pickerell?"

"I guess so," Miss Pickerell said.

Wilbur went on. "Gravity is always strongest when things are closest together. The hardest part of getting away from the earth is right at first. That's why we had to use such a tremendous amount of power for our take-off."

"Was *that* what it was!" Miss Pickerell said. "I thought it was an explosion."

"It was, in a way," Wilbur said. "You see, this whole ship is really a rocket, a sort of giant jet engine. The fuel explodes and escapes through the exhaust nozzle, with a tremendous thrust. That furnishes the power, because the ship has to shoot forward to balance the backward thrust."

"Oh," said Miss Pickerell, who didn't understand this at all. "Is there only one engine? I've always heard that one-engine planes aren't very safe."

"This is quite different," Wilbur said. "There is one main jet. But we have some auxiliary rockets too, to use in turning the ship."

"I see." Miss Pickerell was trying to be polite.

Wilbur went on. "The more powerful the fuel is, the more powerful is the thrust of the exhaust, and the faster the ship goes. This is the only type of engine that is capable of taking us to—"

"MR. KILLIAN!" It was the starchy voice of the captain

speaking so loud that Wilbur and Miss Pickerell had no difficulty in hearing it from the other room. "Is it too much to ask you, Mr. Killian, to render an opinion? You have had a number of minutes to study the instruments. *Are* we on our course, or are we not?"

Miss Pickerell looked at Wilbur. "Can't the captain tell if we're on our course or not?"

"Oh, no," Wilbur said. "You see, he's not really a captain."

"He's not!"

"No. Captain Crandall is really a lecturer and an explorer. He makes trips to strange places, and when he comes back he gives travel talks."

Wilbur stopped as they heard Mr. Killian say, "It's the instruments, Captain. They're all out of whack. Can't tell a thing by them."

"Oh, good gracious!" they heard Captain Crandall say. Then he shouted, "Wilbur! Where in the world have you gone! Come here immediately!"

"I have to go," Wilbur said. "Excuse me, Miss Pickerell." He swam to the opening and disappeared.

"This whole expedition is the most ridiculous thing I have ever heard of," Miss Pickerell said to herself, "and I'm going right out there and tell the captain so."

10. THE CAPTAIN IS BAFFLED

BUT WHEN she floated out into the other room and saw the men at the instrument panel, Miss Pickerell changed her mind.

Mr. Killian floated back and forth, from one end of the panel to the other, turning knobs and adjusting dials and pulling levers. Wilbur, under the captain's direction, was removing screws from one of the instruments on the panel. It had a large round dial. The captain, suspended in the air behind them, kept barking at Mr. Killian, and Mr. Killian kept answering in monosyllables. Miss Pickerell decided this would be a poor time to engage the captain in conversation.

"He sounds so cross," she thought. And then she thought, "Maybe he's hungry. Perhaps all of them are hungry." Miss Pickerell suddenly realized that she was hungry herself. And no wonder. She hadn't even had her supper.

She would get supper for the men. Then perhaps the captain would be in a more conversational mood.

Miss Pickerell straightened her apron and looked around for the kitchen.

But she could see nothing that looked like food, or a place to prepare food. She began to wonder. Perhaps all their food was in liquid form. Perhaps they pumped food into their mouths the way Wilbur had pumped her drink of water.

As she started to swim over to the panel and ask the

men about this, she saw that Wilbur had finished unscrewing the instrument with the large round dial.

"There!" he said, as he carefully handed it to Captain Crandall.

The captain took it and swam with it to his own compartment. At the opening he paused to say, "I may not be able to make rapid calculations the way Mr. Haggerty can, but there's one thing I know how to do. I know how to calibrate electronic instruments."

Miss Pickerell was just about to ask the captain what calibrating meant, when Mr. Killian said, "A good thing, too! Can't even tell if we're on our course until the instruments are recalibrated—until they give the correct readings."

The captain looked at the dial of the instrument in his hand. "It reads 32 now," he said to Mr. Killian. "What should it say?"

Mr. Killian consulted a scale printed on the instrument panel. "When it's properly calibrated," he said, "it ought to read 24."

Miss Pickerell could see that calibrating an electronic instrument, to make it give the correct reading, must be something like regulating a clock, to make it tell the correct time.

Captain Crandall retired to his compartment.

Miss Pickerell remembered the second opening in the partition—the one Wilbur had come floating out of just after the flight started. Perhaps the cans of liquid food were in there. She propelled herself through the opening. This compartment proved to be what she was looking for.

One whole wall of this room was a cupboard. Through the transparent doors, Miss Pickerell saw quantities of food, not stacked up, but just suspended in space. Many of the items were inside little wire baskets or plastic boxes. Miss Pickerell noticed several large purple boxes of pretzels.

Deciding to set the table first, Miss Pickerell looked around for it, but all she saw was a long board in the center of the room, fitted with clamps and wire baskets held upside down. Miss Pickerell lifted one of the baskets by the edge. It appeared to be held to the board by a spring clamp, for when she released the basket, it snapped back into place.

Suddenly Miss Pickerell laughed at herself. Setting the table, indeed! She saw now that the clamps and wire baskets must be to hold the food in place while the men were eating. Otherwise the food would be all over the room, with no gravity to hold it down.

Miss Pickerell studied the board. It looked very bare. She wished she had some way to make it more attractive. She wished she had some flowers, or some nice linen.

She had an idea.

Taking off her apron, Miss Pickerell laid it across the board and fastened it under four of the clamps. "There!" she said, "That will make it seem more homelike."

From the cupboard she selected some apples, some cans with tubes and pumps labeled "Soup," "Iced Tea," "Hot Coffee," a large meat loaf already cut into slices and held together in a basket, and some pretzels from one of the large purple boxes. These she placed under the wire baskets on the table.

Then she floated to the door of the compartment and called out cheerily, "Supper's ready!"

Captain Crandall, the instrument in his hand, emerged from his compartment. For the first time since she had seen him, the captain looked almost pleasant.

"I've fixed it, men," he said. "I've recalibrated the instrument. It now gives the correct reading." He pointed to the dial, and Miss Pickerell, looking down over his head, saw that the needle on the dial now pointed to 24.

"Come on, men," Captain Crandall said. "We might as well eat. There isn't much we can do now, until I get the rest of the instruments recalibrated."

He started into the compartment where the food was, and then he floated back to allow Miss Pickerell to precede him. But all he said was, "I'm glad to see you're making yourself useful around here, Miss. . . ."

"Pickerell," said Wilbur, who was right behind them.

"Miss Pickerell. I see you've found a tablecloth."

"It's just my apron," Miss Pickerell said, but she was glad the captain had noticed.

Mr. Killian came in through the opening.

Miss Pickerell said, "Now, you men just sit right down —I mean, just hang on. . . . Well, anyway, you just start eating. And Captain Crandall, as soon as you're through eating, I want to talk to you."

Wilbur came up behind her. "Just hang on to the edge of the table, Miss Pickerell, and I'll fasten a strap around you."

Captain Crandall gravely took his place at the table opposite Miss Pickerell. He very carefully placed the instrument under an empty wire basket.

Miss Pickerell ate the same way the men were doing, by holding the food close to her mouth with both hands. She could see that knives and forks would be of no use, for the food, instead of stopping at their mouths, would go right up over their heads.

Captain Crandall ate more than anyone else. Miss Pickerell had already decided, because of his plump face, that he must be a man who enjoyed his food. As soon as she was sure he was quite through, she said, "Now, then, Captain Crandall—"

"*Just* a minute, Miss . . . Pickerell. *I'm* the captain of this ship. I'll do the talking."

"Well, Captain, it's just that I'd like to know definitely just when this trip will be over."

"Probably never," Mr. Killian mumbled.

Miss Pickerell paid no attention. "I have things to do at home. I've been away for a month already. Besides that, my cow is not well, though I don't worry too much about her. Mr. Haggerty told me himself that he loved farm animals and always wanted to be a veterinarian, so I'm sure he will look out for my cow, but I really must insist on getting back home in time to prepare my collection of rocks for the state fair. . . . Why, what's the matter, Captain?"

The captain's face had turned ashen white, as he reached into the inverted basket where he had placed the instrument he had recalibrated. He pointed. The needle on the dial had gone back to 32 again.

Slowly, Captain Crandall looked up, holding the eyes of each man in turn.

"If I didn't know it was impossible," he said, "if I

didn't know that you men understand the delicacy of electronic instruments and realize how responsive electronic instruments are to magnetic fields—I would say that someone had brought a magnet on board this ship."

11. MISS PICKERELL MAKES SUGGESTIONS

O H, IS that all that's the trouble!" Miss Pickerell said brightly. "Captain, you should have said so before. There *is* a magnet on board. It's my magnetic hammer. It's in the pocket of my apron on the table right there in front of you."

Captain Crandall bent his head into the palm of his hand, and groaned. Then, holding the instrument out as far as he could with one hand, he reached into the apron pocket and removed the magnetic hammer.

"Here," he said, handing it to Mr. Killian. "Take this and fasten it somewhere where it can't move, so its effect on the instruments will remain constant."

"I think that's rather silly," Miss Pickerell said. "In the first place, it is very hard for me to see how such a little thing as my magnetic hammer could make all that difference in the instruments. But if it does, let's just get rid of it. Then you wouldn't need to recalibrate the other instruments. Of course, it is my favorite hammer. But I can probably buy another one."

Captain Crandall groaned again.

"Here," Miss Pickerell said to Mr. Killian. "Let me have it. I'll get rid of it."

Mr. Killian made no move to give her the hammer. "How?" he inquired.

"Why, I'll just open the door and throw it out. Or course, it would be easier to throw it out a window, but

"Fasten this where it can't move," said the captain

I notice there aren't any windows. If I were building a space ship, I'd put in some windows so people could see where they're going."

"Miss Pickerell," Captain Crandall said, "do you know anything at all about atmospheric pressure?"

"No," said Miss Pickerell. "What is that?"

"It is the pressure, or weight, of the earth's atmosphere. All of our lives we have lived with the earth's atmosphere above us. We have become conditioned to its pressure. We cannot live otherwise."

"Very interesting," Miss Pickerell said. "However—"

"Kindly do not interrupt me, Miss Pickerell! There is another thing necessary to our lives. We have to have oxygen to breathe."

"I know that!" Miss Pickerell said.

"In space, there is no oxygen, no atmosphere, and, of course, no atmospheric pressure. This space ship has been constructed with that in mind. Oxygen is provided for us to breathe, and a pressure is maintained equal to what we are used to. That calls for very strong construction. That is why there are no windows to weaken the walls."

"Oh," said Miss Pickerell. "And if I opened the door, I might let out some of the oxygen?"

"You couldn't open the door," the captain said, "because it's sealed with a pressure lock. And I can't take any more time to explain things to you, since I have to calibrate all the instruments again, when I had planned to be working on my speech all this time instead." He sighed wearily. "Come on, men."

"What speech?" Miss Pickerell asked.

But the captain seemed not to have heard. Miss Pickerell put away the food and removed her apron from the table. She was about to put it on when Wilbur returned.

"Here, Miss Pickerell," he said. "I'll tie it for you." He tied the apron strings in a neat bow in the middle of Miss Pickerell's back.

"Why don't you try to get some sleep, Miss Pickerell?" Wilbur said as they floated out into the main room.

"I am sleepy," Miss Pickerell admitted.

"And be sure to pull that netting down over the top of your bunk, so you won't float away if you should turn over in your sleep." Miss Pickerell started to untie her apron.

"You don't need to take it off," Wilbur said. "It won't get wrinkled."

Miss Pickerell, stretched out flat on the surface of her bunk, did not go to sleep immediately, in spite of her drowsiness. She lay perfectly still, thinking about this amazing experience of hers. How surprised her nieces and nephews would be when they learned that she had actually had a ride in a space ship. She decided that she would call them up by long-distance, the minute the space ship landed.

Miss Pickerell turned over. She bounced softly against the netting above her, almost as if she were a balloon. When she pushed herself back, she noticed that her body made no dent in the cushions of the bunk. She lay there, without weight, barely touching the surface below her. Miss Pickerell slept.

12. MISS PICKERELL MAKES
A DISCOVERY

WHEN Miss Pickerell awoke, it was with a guilty start. She had just remembered that the governor was going to telephone her. The governor would think her inexcusably rude when he called and no one answered.

Miss Pickerell did not know what time it was, but from the delightfully rested feeling of her body, she was sure she must have slept the whole night through. She would get up and get breakfast, and then explain to Captain Crandall that she really had to get back, on account of the governor's telephone call.

But it was to be many days before Miss Pickerell had a chance to talk to Captain Crandall. It took him all that time to get the whole bank of instruments corrected. Day after day the captain worked. His blue eyes grew bleary. His plump red face became thin and pale. He had Wilbur bring his meals to him in his own compartment. Miss Pickerell began to wonder if he ever slept at all.

Sometimes the captain worked directly at the instrument panel, and during those times, when his own compartment was empty, Miss Pickerell would sometimes go in there, just for a change of scene, for frankly she was beginning to find the trip very boring.

One day she remembered about the automatic camera. She remembered that she wanted to see how her farm looked from up in the air. She went to the side of the machine where, by this time quite a large stack of colored photographs had accumulated inside the mesh container. Miss Pickerell reached inside the netting and pulled out the latest photograph.

At first, she didn't understand what she was looking at. It took her several minutes to realize that the colored ball, or globe, pictured here must actually be the earth.

"Why, it's beautiful!" she said. "The earth is beautiful!" She pulled herself down into the captain's chair and snapped the belt across her lap to hold her in place while she leaned forward to study the picture.

At opposite ends of the earth, she saw irregular caps of white, one larger than the other. These, she knew, must be the polar areas. It was the ice and snow that made them look so white. Between these two white caps, the earth showed a great variety of colors. There were extensive areas of green, shading all the way from dark to light and back again. The darker areas, she supposed, were forests, and the lighter ones, plains or meadows.

Miss Pickerell was puzzled by a large irregular mass of red, until she finally decided it must be one of the great deserts of the world. The very dark areas, which were so large, Miss Pickerell had no difficulty in recognizing as the oceans.

Miss Pickerell was just a little frightened, when she realized how very high they had come. She hoped the captain could get the instruments corrected soon, so they could find their course and turn around and go home again.

The next day she asked the captain to give her something to do. "I'll feel very silly," she said, "when my nieces and nephews ask me, 'And what did you do on the trip?' and all I'll be able to tell them is that I got the meals."

Captain Crandall looked at her out of his tired eyes. "There's nothing you can do to help *me*," he said. "However, if Mr. Killian wants to use you as an assistant, I shan't object. It's only because we are shorthanded, however. I don't believe in giving responsibility to stowaways."

"Oh, thank you, Captain Crandall. I feel more useful already." She presented herself to Mr. Killian at the instrument panel.

Mr. Killian seemed doubtful, at first, that he could find anything for Miss Pickerell to do. But when she insisted, he finally gave her an assignment.

"Come over here," he said, indicating the eyepiece of what looked to Miss Pickerell like some sort of periscope. She looked into the eyepiece.

"Oh!" she exclaimed. "How beautiful! Millions of stars! And the sky is perfectly black. I suppose that means it's the middle of the night."

"Space always looks dark," Mr. Killian said. "No atmosphere to catch the sun's rays. Now, do you see where two thin white lines cross?"

Miss Pickerell said, "Yes."

"And you see a bright, blue-looking star just where the two lines come together?"

"Yes."

"All right. Just keep watching. As long as the bright

blue star and those white lines are together, we know where we are. We may not know where we're going—at least, until the instruments are fixed—but we know where we are. If we drift, if we lose the bright blue star, or it moves away from the two lines, call me."

Keeping her eye on the bright blue star and trying to focus on the white lines where they crossed was very hard on Miss Pickerell's eyes. It made them water, and she took turns, looking first through one eye and then through the other. But she was very faithful to her duties. She insisted on standing watch, just as Wilbur and Mr. Killian did, and as the days went by, she maintained her vigil of the bright blue star.

It made her feel important. She felt like Columbus. This would really be something to tell her nieces and nephews—how she had kept the ship on its course while the captain recalibrated the instruments.

Never for more than a moment did Miss Pickerell relax her study of the blue star and the intersecting white lines, so long as she was on duty.

Once, however, in the process of changing from one eye to the other, she allowed herself a quick glance around the heavens. She could scarcely believe what she saw!

Just coming into view at one side of the eyepiece was a small red globe. It wasn't so much its size—although that was much greater than the stars—that startled Miss Pickerell. What astounded her was its color of dusky red. She remembered that Mars had looked red when she had seen it through the telescope at the state fair. She also remembered that, early in the flight, the captain had claimed he was headed for Mars. Even Mr. Haggerty, before the flight began, had hinted at such a thing.

Was this red globe Mars? Could it be possible that they *were* going to Mars after all?

13. DESTINATION MARS

A STRANGE change took place in Miss Pickerell. All this time she had been wanting to get home to her cow and her rock collection. She had been impatient. She had been bored. She had looked forward to nothing but her return to the earth.

Now, however, she suddenly found herself wanting to go on. She no longer wished to go back. She felt a wild excitement of anticipation. Miss Pickerell knew now how explorers must feel. She almost ached with eagerness. She felt that if they couldn't somehow get to Mars, the disappointment would be so great she wouldn't be able to stand it.

"That *is* Mars, isn't it?" she asked Mr. Killian hopefully, when he came to relieve her at the eyepiece.

"Oh, sure," said Mr. Killian.

Miss Pickerell sighed with relief. "About how far away would you say it was, Mr. Killian?"

"About 10 or 15 million miles," Mr. Killian said airily.

"Oh. . . . Well, then, I suppose it will be quite a little while before we get there."

"*If* we ever do!"

"You mean we might run out of—out of fuel?" Miss Pickerell was alarmed.

"Don't have to worry about that. Using atomic fuel."

"Oh, good!" said Miss Pickerell. She remained hovering in the air behind Mr. Killian, too excited to go back

67

to her bunk and rest. "As long as Mars is in such plain sight, why can't we just point the ship directly at it?"

"Wouldn't work," Mr. Killian said. "On account of the orbit. You know about orbits?"

"I know the earth has an orbit," Miss Pickerell said. "I know that the earth travels around the sun. And I know it takes the earth a whole year to go all the way around its orbit."

"Mars does the same thing," Mr. Killian said. "All the planets do. All the planets move in orbits around the sun. Some of them have bigger orbits because they are farther away from the sun. And some of them take longer."

"How long does it take Mars to go around its orbit?" Miss Pickerell asked.

"Almost twice as long as the earth takes. Mars is farther away from the sun than the earth is."

Miss Pickerell thought about this for a minute. "Mr. Killian. If the earth is moving all the time in an orbit, and if Mars is moving all the time in its orbit, then, at this very minute, we must be right between the earth's orbit and Mars' orbit."

"That's right."

"I begin to understand now," Miss Pickerell said. "Of course we can't point the ship right at Mars, because by the time we got where Mars is now, Mars would be somewhere else—somewhere else along its orbit."

"Sure. Another thing makes it complicated. An orbit isn't round. More like a hoop that's been squeezed in on two sides."

"Dear me!" Miss Pickerell said. "It *is* very complicated, isn't it? Oh, I *do* hope we'll be able to figure out just the right place to steer toward, so that this ship and Mars will get there at the same time."

"Nobody could do that but Haggerty," Mr. Killian said, "because we're moving so fast ourselves. This ship has a sort of orbit, too. Only hope is that the original calculations were correct."

Their suspense about the original calculations came to an end that very day, when the last of the instruments had been recalibrated and reset into the panel.

Mr. Killian made a number of adjustments, and the captain hovered right behind him.

"Well," the captain asked. "What about it, Mr. Killian? Are we on our course? Will we get to Mars?"

Mr. Killian moved away from the panel and referred to a chart fastened to the wall. He returned and took readings from the instruments.

"Yes," he said. "We're on our course, sir. We'll get to Mars all right."

"Oh, good!" Miss Pickerell said, pressing her hands tightly together.

The captain turned and looked at her oddly. "I was under the impression, Miss Pickerell, that you wanted to get home as fast as possible."

"Oh, well!" Miss Pickerell said. "That was before. I didn't think such a thing was possible then. But now—why, now I wouldn't miss going to Mars for anything in the world. I don't even mind if we get back too late for the state fair."

"We will," Mr. Killian said. "Much too late."

14. MISS PICKERELL HAS AN IDEA

NOW THAT they knew they were on their course, everyone relaxed. There was little to do, Miss Pickerell was told, until it was time to make a landing on Mars.

Mr. Killian slept a great deal. Wilbur spent a good deal of time studying a large loose-leaf notebook, and Miss Pickerell, having found a ball of light string in a cupboard, occupied herself by crocheting with the crochet hook that Wilbur had made for her out of a piece of wire.

The captain kept to his compartment and worked on his lecture.

One day Miss Pickerell remembered the automatic camera. She wondered if they were close enough now for Mars to show on the pictures. She floated out of her bunk, pushing her crochet work into the pocket of her apron, and went to the captain's compartment.

"Excuse me, Captain, for interrupting you—"

"Yes, yes," said the captain impatiently. "What is it?" He was strapped into his adjustable chair, writing with a blue pencil. At one side of his chair a large clamp held down a number of written pages.

"I just wanted to see if the camera had taken any pictures of Mars."

"Well, hurry up," the captain said, gesturing to the camera. "Take one of the pictures and go away."

Miss Pickerell reached into the mesh container and removed the latest picture. She took it back to her bunk, and sat down to study it. Mr. Killian woke up just then, and he floated out of his bunk and hovered in the air above Miss Pickerell, looking down over her shoulder.

Mars showed itself to be a reddish globe, with white caps at opposite sides, just like those on the earth. Almost all the rest of the globe was reddish in color, though there were a few thin green areas near the base of the white caps. Miss Pickerell remembered the reddish area on the picture of the earth that she had decided must be a large desert.

"Is Mars a desert?" she asked Mr. Killian.

"Probably. Very little water."

"But if there's no water, or very little, how can plants grow?"

"Maybe there aren't any," Mr. Killian said.

This was hard for Miss Pickerell to imagine. It was hard to think of a world in which plants didn't grow.

"But wouldn't plants get water when it rains?"

"Probably doesn't rain on Mars."

"What a very strange place Mars must be!" Miss Pickerell said. "What else is it like, Mr. Killian?"

"Rocks, dust, wind."

"Will it be cold on Mars? Will I need to wear my sweater?"

"Terribly cold," Mr. Killian said. "Especially at night."

"But doesn't the sun shine on Mars and make it warm, just the way the sun shines on the earth?"

"Mars' atmosphere is too thin to hold the heat in.

Heat all goes away as soon as the sun goes down.

The captain appeared at the door of his compartment. "Well, Mr. Killian," he said. "Have you nothing better to do than look at colored pictures?"

"No," Mr. Killian said. "I guess not, sir."

"We are getting closer to Mars all the time," the captain said. "I should think you would be planning our landing."

"Landing!" Mr. Killian's voice sounded frightened. "*I* don't know how to make a landing on a strange planet. All I know is take-offs. Haggerty was supposed to do the landing."

The captain looked at Wilbur, who had been studying his notebook as he sat in his bunk.

"Not me!" Wilbur said. His eyes looked terrified. "I've never even *been* in a space ship before. All I know about space flight is the things I've read and studied. I just came along for the practical experience."

"You'll get experience, all right!" Mr. Killian said gloomily.

Miss Pickerell could stand it no longer.

"Captain Crandall," she said, "I can't resist saying that this is one of the most poorly prepared expeditions I have ever heard of."

"Aren't you forgetting something, Miss Pickerell?" the captain said coldly. "Aren't you forgetting that if it hadn't been for you, Mr. Haggerty would be with us at this very moment?"

"Oh. . . . Yes. . . . Well. . . . Now the thing to do," Miss Pickerell said, "is not to get panicky. There must be some way we can land the ship, if we just use our common sense."

"You have some specific suggestions, Miss Pickerell?" the captain asked.

"Well," Miss Pickerell said slowly. She tried to think. She remembered what Wilbur had told her about the workings of gravity.

"Does Mars have gravity?" she asked.

"Not as much as the earth," the captain said. "The gravity of Mars is only about a third the gravity of the earth."

"Oh." Miss Pickerell was disappointed. "I thought for a minute that maybe we could just turn off the power and let gravity pull us down. But if Mars' gravity is only one third as strong as the earth's gravity, maybe it would be too weak. . . . And anyway, we couldn't land head-on."

"That's obvious," the captain said.

"And we can't land flat," Miss Pickerell continued, "because we have to be able to take off again. I remember that we took off from the earth pointing straight up."

"Exactly," said the captain. "Come on, men. Let's go into my compartment and figure this thing out scientifically." He started to swim toward his compartment, and then he turned around.

"Wait a minute," he said. "Maybe we can use Miss Pickerell's suggestion after all. What we'll do is try to turn the ship around as we approach Mars' gravitational field. Then we'll use just enough forward power to balance the pull of Mars. That way we'll sort of settle down gradually, and be in the proper position for our take-off."

"Does anyone know how to turn the ship around?" Miss Pickerell was skeptical.

"It tells how to do that right here in this notebook," Wilbur said. "We'll use the auxiliary rockets, but we won't use all of them. Just the ones on one side of the ship. That will—"

"I know," said Miss Pickerell. "It'll be just like turning a rowboat around by using only one oar. Oh, I'm so glad we're going to be able to land! I'm so excited! I can just hardly wait until we get to Mars."

15. DESERTED

MUCH to Miss Pickerell's surprise, their approach to Mars was rather unexciting.

From inside the space ship, there was no way of telling where they were, or even in which direction they were pointing, except by looking through the eyepiece. And Miss Pickerell was now denied this privilege. The men divided the watches between themselves, and carefully rehearsed each step of their landing procedure.

Miss Pickerell spent much time in her bunk, either sitting up crocheting, or lying down sleeping.

Once, when she awoke, she could tell by the tenseness of the men that something important was happening. Wilbur was pulling levers and punching buttons. Mr. Killian was faithfully studying the instruments. The captain was at the eyepiece.

"You've done it, Wilbur," the captain said finally in a low voice. "You've turned us around. Now Mars is beginning to draw us down."

Very shortly, Miss Pickerell began to notice strange sensations in her body. No one had prepared her for the effect of Mars' gravity, and as they came closer and closer, Miss Pickerell grew heavier and heavier in her body, and more and more sluggish in her mind. She noticed that her body sank lower into the cushions of her bunk. It became an effort to turn over. She slept a great deal.

"This is it!" she heard someone shout. "We're here! We've landed."

With great effort, Miss Pickerell managed to turn her heavy head in the direction of the men.

Wilbur and Mr. Killian were standing upright, close together, clapping each other on the back. The captain stood slightly apart, and each man in turn took his hand and shook it solemnly and respectfully.

Miss Pickerell tried to sit up, but she couldn't. She seemed to weigh tons. She lacked the strength to move her heavy body.

"Help!" she called. "I can't move! I'm paralyzed!"

"No, you aren't, Miss Pickerell," Wilbur said, as he walked toward her with tired-seeming steps. "It just seems that way because we've been without gravity for so long. As soon as you get used to it, you'll feel wonderful. You'll feel a lot lighter than you did on earth."

Wilbur was right. Very soon, Miss Pickerell was able to sit up. She stepped down to the floor of the room. It was a strange sensation to be using her leg muscles again after such a long time of floating through the air.

"Well," she said to the captain who was looking across the room at her. "What are we waiting for? Let's open the door and go out."

The captain walked slowly toward her.

"Now, Miss Pickerell," he said. "I expect you to be reasonable about this and not make a fuss. I cannot allow you to leave the ship."

"If you think for one minute, Captain Crandall, that I am going to come all the way to Mars without getting out to see what it's like, you are very much mistaken."

She reached into her bunk for her pink sweater and began to put it on.

The captain said, "Do you see those bulky suits with transparent helmets that the men are putting on? Those are pressure suits. Each person who leaves the ship must wear one, in order to remain alive."

"I don't mind," Miss Pickerell said. "I'll wear Mr. Haggerty's suit. Which one is his?"

"Now, listen, Miss Pickerell—"

"Couldn't she come, Captain?" Wilbur asked. "I'll watch out for her."

"No," Captain Crandall said firmly. "This is a scientific expedition. We are explorers. We cannot be watching out for tourists."

"But, Captain Crandall," Miss Pickerell said, "that's not fair. Don't you remember that it was I who—"

"I remember that it was you who came on board our ship, when you weren't supposed to, and that if you hadn't done so, we would have had Mr. Haggerty with us."

"But you didn't need Mr. Haggerty—as it turned out," Miss Pickerell said.

"That's beside the point. I cannot take the responsibility of letting you leave the ship. However, you may listen to our conversation on the walkie-talkie set. All of our pressure suits have walkie-talkies connected to one in my compartment. You can hear everything that we say to each other, and if you get too lonely, you may speak to us."

"Thank you," Miss Pickerell said stiffly. "That will be a great pleasure, I am sure!" She decided not to argue with the captain any more at present. She would wait until he had returned. Perhaps he would be more approachable then.

She watched the men getting ready to leave the ship. Each man put on a bulky looking suit and fastened a transparent helmet over his head. Inside each helmet was a small microphone just in front of the man's mouth.

Wilbur kept his helmet off till the last, so that he could explain things to Miss Pickerell.

He told her about the atmospheric pressure of Mars—how it was much less than that of the earth. He explained that for that reason the pressure suits must maintain the same pressure as that of the earth. He told her how the atmosphere of Mars did not contain enough oxygen. He showed her the oxygen tanks. Each man carried one of these tanks in a large pocket on the back of his suit. Wilbur showed Miss Pickerell how the oxygen tank was connected to the suit. Also he explained that the temperature of Mars, during most of the day and all of the night, would be far too cold for comfort or safety, which was why the suits were heated.

Then he took her to the door of the ship and explained the pressure lock to her. Mr. Killian was just entering the lock. Miss Pickerell wouldn't have known it was Mr. Killian if he hadn't turned around so that she could see his face through the transparent front of the helmet. In the bulky brown suits, the men looked just alike.

"See, Miss Pickerell," Wilbur said. "He opens the inside door of the pressure lock and goes in. He closes the door and adjusts the pressure valve. The outside door of the lock won't open until the pressure in there is the same as that outside. Do you understand, Miss Pickerell?"

"Not very well," Miss Pickerell said. "But it's nice of you to try to explain it to me, Wilbur."

The last person to leave the ship, the last person to go through the pressure lock, was the captain. "We won't be gone long, Miss Pickerell," he said. He was talking into his microphone because he had already fastened his helmet. It sounded strange to hear his voice coming out of the walkie-talkie in the captain's compartment behind Miss Pickerell, when she could see his lips moving as he stood directly in front of her.

"We'll be back within half an hour," the captain said. "Half an hour at the most." Then he stepped into the pressure lock and closed the inside door.

Miss Pickerell was left alone.

16. MISS PICKERELL TO THE RESCUE

ALMOST immediately, Miss Pickerell heard the voice of the captain coming from the walkie-talkie in his compartment.

"Miss Pickerell," he said. "Did I leave my watch in there?"

Miss Pickerell hurried into the captain's compartment. The watch was on a bench. She noticed that it was just half past twelve.

"Yes, Captain," she said, stooping to speak into the microphone on a bench before the captain's chair. "I'll bring it to you. I'll put on Mr. Haggerty's suit and bring it right out."

"Miss Pickerell," the captain said in his customary sharp voice, "you are to remain on the ship. Those are my orders. I merely wanted to be sure that my watch was there. Do not leave the ship under any circumstances."

Miss Pickerell did not answer. The captain had no right to talk to her like that. He had no right to give her orders. She was not a member of his crew. If she chose to get out and see what Mars looked like, he had no authority to prevent it. She went back to where Mr. Haggerty's pressure suit was lying in an open chest. She reached down to pick it up, but then she changed her mind.

"I suppose it would be wrong," she said. "I suppose

Something must have happened to his walkie-talkie

it would be more honest to wait until the captain gives me permission to go outside."

She went back and sat down in the captain's chair. From time to time she heard the men speaking into their microphones.

Sometimes they addressed remarks to her and she answered them. "Don't tell me what it's like," she said. "I want to see for myself, when the captain lets me go out."

"I'll bring you a souvenir, Miss Pickerell." It was Wilbur's voice. "How would you like a rock?"

"A rock!" Miss Pickerell exclaimed. "Are there rocks right out there?"

"All kinds," Wilbur said. "Red, mostly. They're very pretty. I'll bring you one."

Now Miss Pickerell was twice as eager to get outside. Red rocks from Mars would make a wonderful addition to her rock collection at home.

"Come back, Wilbur." This was the captain's voice. "You're getting too far away from us."

"All right," Wilbur said. "I'm just getting a red rock for Miss Pickerell."

"Miss Pickerell. What time is it?" the captain asked.

Miss Pickerell looked at the captain's watch. "It's a quarter to one," she said.

"All right, men," the captain said. "Everybody turn around and go back to the ship. We'll run out of oxygen if we stay away any longer."

Miss Pickerell heard Wilbur's voice. "Captain, something's happened. I'm stuck. My foot is caught between two big rocks. Help me, Captain."

Miss Pickerell listened for the captain's answer. "Here we come, Miss Pickerell," was all he said.

"Captain!" Miss Pickerell shrieked. Something must have happened to his walkie-talkie. He must not have heard Wilbur's call.

Miss Pickerell remembered that once before this had happened. On the very first day of the flight, when Wilbur had tried to report her from the pasture gate to the space ship, the walkie-talkie had been out of order at first.

Again she heard Wilbur's voice. "Please, Captain. I need help."

"What is it, Miss Pickerell?" said the captain's voice. "Is anything the mat—" There was a sharp click and complete silence. The walkie-talkie had gone dead. Miss Pickerell shouted into the mouthpiece, but there was no answer from the captain, or from Wilbur, or from Mr. Killian.

For seconds, Miss Pickerell sat there, stiff with horror. Unless the captain turned around, he would never know that Wilbur was not right behind him. Wilbur would run out of oxygen. . . .

"Wilbur," Miss Pickerell said, just in case he was still able to hear her voice. "Don't be frightened! I'm coming. I'm coming to help you."

She dashed to where she had left Mr. Haggerty's pressure suit. She picked it up. It was clumsy and heavy. She struggled into it, one foot at a time. She had no time to take off her clothes, and her skirts made a bulky wad around her waist. She took an oxygen tank and put it into the big loose pocket on the back of the suit. She lifted the helmet over her head and fastened it, though this was hard to do because of the thick gloves that sealed the ends of her sleeves.

Last of all, Miss Pickerell connected the oxygen tank to its opening in the suit, the way Wilbur had showed her. She hurried to the pressure lock, but just before she entered it, she went back and gathered up another oxygen tank in her arms. This would be for Wilbur in case he ran out of oxygen before they could free his foot.

Inside the pressure lock, she closed the inner door. She remembered Wilbur had said something about adjusting the pressure valve. In the wall of the lock was a small handle and Miss Pickerell turned this. Immediately there was a hoarse sucking sound, and in a few moments, Miss Pickerell was able to open the outer door.

She almost fainted when she saw how high above the ground she was. There was a thin ladder leading down to the red rocky waste below, and she would have to descend this, wearing the bulky pressure suit, and carrying the extra tank of oxygen for Wilbur.

But Miss Pickerell did not hesitate. Somehow, slipping and clutching at each rung, and keeping her eyes tight closed to fight against her dizziness, somehow, she managed to get to the ground. She opened her eyes.

Far in the distance, she could see Wilbur. He was alternately waving his arms in the air, and stooping down to try to free his trapped foot.

Between Wilbur and the space ship, and coming toward her, Miss Pickerell saw the other men. Neither one had missed Wilbur. Apparently each man thought Wilbur was following behind.

Clutching the extra oxygen tank, Miss Pickerell lumbered toward the men. It was hard to walk in the heavy suit. The ground was rough and rocky, and now and then strong gusts of wind blew thick clouds of red dust across the front of her helmet.

She waved and pointed, trying to make the men turn around and look back. But this only made them walk faster. As they neared each other, Miss Pickerell could identify the face of the captain in the lead. He took long angry steps and his blue eyes were blazing. His lips, inside the transparent helmet, were moving, and although Miss Pickerell could not tell what he was saying, she knew he must be expressing his indignation at her for defying his orders about leaving the ship.

"Captain!" she shouted. "Captain!" If only the walkie-talkie would work.

The captain had almost reached her now. He tried to take hold of her arm, but Miss Pickerell squirmed away. She said the word "Wilbur" over and over, stretching her lips wide each time, hoping that the captain would understand.

Then she suddenly grasped the captain by the sleeve of his suit and partly turned him around. She pointed again, and this time the captain saw.

The captain hesitated for only a second. Very quickly and deftly he disconnected his oxygen tank and substituted it for the one Miss Pickerell was wearing. After he had connected the tank he had been wearing to her suit, he took the extra tank from her arms and hurried out across the rocks toward Wilbur.

Miss Pickerell started to follow, but a gentle pull re-

strained her. It was Mr. Killian. Miss Pickerell turned back toward the ship. She realized that the captain's depleted tank of oxygen would not take her far. She would have to go back and wait inside the ship until the captain and Wilbur returned.

Mr. Killian gestured that she was to climb the ladder and enter the pressure lock. From the top of the ladder, Miss Pickerell took one look back. She had the satisfaction of seeing that the captain had reached Wilbur. With one powerful tug, he freed Wilbur's trapped foot, and the two men stood together a moment while the captain connected the extra oxygen tank to Wilbur's suit. Then, as Miss Pickerell stooped through the outer door of the pressure lock, they hurried to the ship.

She pointed and this time the captain saw

17. HOME AGAIN

FROM that day on, nothing was too good for Miss Pickerell. Mr. Killian, who still addressed the others in short, choppy sentences, became very talkative with Miss Pickerell, and told her the complete story of his life, bit by bit. Wilbur waited on Miss Pickerell hand and foot. And the captain, even before he began repairing the walkie-talkie set, made her a stiff little speech of apology.

"I have misjudged you, Miss Pickerell. I hope you will forgive my abruptness to you earlier in the flight. I doubt very much if even Mr. Haggerty could have thought and acted as quickly as you did to save Wilbur's life. It is an honor to have you as a member of our expedition."

Now, each time any of the men went outside, Miss Pickerell was allowed, and even urged, to accompany them. She made so many trips up and down the ladder between Mars and the space ship that she quite overcame her dizziness, and was never troubled by it again, so long as she lived.

During their stay on Mars, Miss Pickerell had plenty of opportunity to see what the planet was like. She observed that it was dry, rocky, dusty, and flat.

As far as the expedition could tell, there was no animal life on Mars. And Miss Pickerell saw for herself that the only plant life was a sort of dry moss that grew around some of the rocks.

There were no clouds, except dust clouds. There was no rain. Miss Pickerell decided that the earth was a much pleasanter planet than Mars. She was glad she lived on the earth.

However, Miss Pickerell did find many beautiful red rocks on Mars. And the men were so generous about adding to her collection that within a few days her bunk was nearly filled with rocks. There was just a narrow space next to the wall, for Miss Pickerell to sit and lie.

Mars and the earth were different in so many ways that Miss Pickerell was a little surprised to learn that the days on Mars were almost exactly the same length as the days on earth.

"Only thirty-seven minutes longer," Captain Crandall said one day when she asked him about it. "You see, both Mars and the earth are spinning around all the time, just like tops. That's what makes—"

"I know," Miss Pickerell said. "That's what makes night and day."

"And they both spin at just about the same rate. That's why days here on Mars are almost the same length as the days on earth. And by the way, Miss Pickerell, I'd advise you to do something with those rocks of yours before tomorrow. We're going to start home tomorrow, and if you leave your rocks where they are, they'll be all over the place the minute we get away from the gravity of Mars. Maybe Wilbur can show you a chest or cupboard to put them in."

Miss Pickerell kept the seven finest specimens with

her, the ones she was going to give her nieces and nephews for souvenirs, so that she would have something to admire on the trip home. The rest of the rocks she and Wilbur locked away inside a chest.

When it was time for the take-off, Miss Pickerell strapped herself firmly back against her bunk, closed her eyes tightly, and prepared herself for the explosion.

This time, too, although she had been determined not to, Miss Pickerell lost consciousness, and wakened to find that once more they were without the pull of gravity.

On the return trip, everyone was excited and happy—even the captain. He kept flitting back and forth between the main room and his own compartment, where he wrote page after page after page with his blue pencil.

"This is going to be one of my finest lectures," he said one day. "And, Miss Pickerell, sometime when I am lecturing in the vicinity of Square Toe Mountain, you must come and sit on the platform with me and let me introduce you to the audience as the first woman who has ever been to Mars. You'll be famous, you know."

"How soon will we be home, Captain Crandall?" Miss Pickerell asked.

"Just a few days more, Miss Pickerell. Aren't you excited?"

"A little," Miss Pickerell admitted. But Miss Pickerell was also worried. The nearer they came to the end of their trip, the more Miss Pickerell worried.

"It's about my cow," she confided to Wilbur. "I should never have left her all alone down there with a strange man. Oh, I do hope she'll be all right."

"You didn't mean to come, Miss Pickerell," Wilbur said. "It was an accident. It wasn't your fault."

"I hope Mr. Haggerty won't be mad at me," Miss Pickerell said, "for coming in his place."

Just then the captain called out from the instrument panel where he and Mr. Killian had been conferring.

"We're approaching the earth now, Miss Pickerell. We're going to have to get used to gravity all over again. Why don't you try to go to sleep while we land?"

Miss Pickerell did go to sleep, and when she woke up, she knew by the heaviness of her body that they had returned. The pull of gravity was more than she could cope with.

Even the men were having trouble moving this time. She saw Wilbur trying to walk along the edge of the room. But he was pulling himself along by using the handholds on the wall, as if he lacked the strength to move otherwise. He reached the pressure lock and opened both doors. A path of sunlight fell across the floor.

Wilbur looked out. "Hi! Haggerty!" he shouted, and Miss Pickerell heard Mr. Haggerty answer him. Then she heard another sound. A welcome sound. She heard the contented mooing of her cow. Miss Pickerell sighed with relief. Now all she had to worry about was apologizing to Mr. Haggerty for taking his place so that he had to stay behind.

By the time they were ready to leave the space ship, Miss Pickerell had begun to regain the use of her arms and legs. She was beginning to get accustomed to her own heaviness again. She stood up.

The captain emerged from the door of his compartment. He crossed to Miss Pickerell's bunk and picked up her pink sweater. He held the sweater for her so that she could slip her arms into the sleeves.

"Captain Crandall," Miss Pickerell said, "promise me one thing. Promise you won't move this space ship out of my pasture until my nieces and nephews have a chance to come and see it."

"I promise," said the captain.

Down on the ground, Miss Pickerell hurried toward Mr. Haggerty and her cow. Mr. Haggerty held the cow's rope in one hand. His other arm lay affectionately along her back. Miss Pickerell could see that the cow was well and happy.

"Miss Pickerell," Mr. Haggerty said, "I just can't thank you enough for—"

"Mr. Haggerty," said Miss Pickerell, "I do want to apologize—"

They both stopped and looked at each other.

"Thank me for what?" Miss Pickerell asked.

"For the chance to take care of your cow," said Mr. Haggerty. "Do you know what I've decided, Miss Pickerell?"

"No," said Miss Pickerell.

"I've decided to go back to college and study to be a veterinarian after all. And it's all because I've had such a good time making your cow well again. I just love farm animals."

"And you're not mad because you didn't get a chance to go to Mars?"

"Certainly not," said Mr. Haggerty. "And by the way,

I have a message for you, Miss Pickerell. I wrote it down and put it in my brief case. My brief case is over there by the fence. It was a telephone message."

"Oh, mercy!" said Miss Pickerell. "Was it from the governor?"

"I remember now," Mr. Haggerty said. "It was from the governor's wife. I told the governor what had happened the day he called you back—the first day of the flight. Then the governor's wife called. She told me to tell you they want you to come and visit in the governor's mansion when you get back. That was what I wrote down in my brief case."

Miss Pickerell stroked her cow's neck. She looked around her beautiful green, sunny pasture. She heard the cow pulling off a mouthful of grass, with a noisy tearing sound.

"It's so good to be home," Miss Pickerell said. "Do you know something, Mr. Haggerty? There isn't even any *grass* on Mars!"

In the next few months, Miss Pickerell made several visits to the governor's mansion. The following year, at the state fair, her collection of red rocks from Mars won not only the blue ribbon, but also the special gold medal given each year for the most outstanding exhibit of the whole fair. The governor himself made the awards. And Mr. Haggerty spent his first college vacation on Miss Pickerell's farm.

In fact, Miss Pickerell's life was never the same as it had been before she went to Mars.

But the biggest change, and the one Miss Pickerell liked the best, was in her nieces and nephews. From the moment she called them up by long-distance and invited them to come and see the space ship in her pasture —from that moment on—her seven nieces and nephews never tired of hearing Miss Pickerell tell them about her wonderful trip. They admired the blue ribbon and the gold medal. And all their lives long, they treasured the souvenirs Miss Pickerell gave them—the seven beautiful red rocks brought from the planet of Mars.